Acknowledgments

***

Yvette Fay Campbell:
You are God sent. I am everything and anything with and because of you. You are absolute purity and generosity and have given me the gift of perseverance and perspective. I have loved you from the womb.

Stanford Nathaniel Campbell:
Thank you for shaping me in your image for the love of language for painting the picture of a MAN. I love you between each moment within every breath.

Vandell DeJuan Esop Campbell:
My little brother; you have taught me courage and responsibility. Your backbone is forged from Iron and steel; Ogun Warrior. I love you always

Ainsley Burrows:
You have ultimately saved my soul and continue to provide inspiration. I would have written this all to the wind if not for you. *Ever grateful brother*

Thank you to countless others:
The 540 Clan: [Vincent, Katika, Brett Mike, Kim, Ali, India and Tep] who gave me spirit and have always been there for me. Natalie Patterson and Lynne Cole you were my oxygen. Ove your heart and passion remind me of why we do this - Zinc reincarnated. Sudeshna [sona] you taught me patience, trust and are the daughter of new beginnings. Kimberly Johnson you are a scorpion's bite passion and tasty poison. Kerri Jeffries Mubarrak you are my mirror tilted to the left and you keep me afloat. Kareen you are my sea scrolls on sacred parchment. Susan, your unwavering support has been a blessing to me. Charles Thompson, thank you for your advice. Abey, you are my dreams in sepia, you have designed my future in your palms. Melanie your smile and laugh are infectious, thank you for your support. Charlene McCoy, nothing would be the same without your presence. The poets and audiences at the Nuyorican Poetry Lounge, Serengeti Plains, Berkeley Slam, Brooklyn Moon, Oakland Slam, Da Poetry Lounge (for making a stranger feel home). You all gave me a forum to share my life. To all my friends who have added to the sum of my experiences. Thank you all forever.

3

Introduction

***

I was one of the 100 monkeys (#37) so I wrote this book to help speed up the process.

***

I have come to the realization that I am simply a vehicle for these words; a vessel to remind us of journeys forgotten eons ago. My hope is that this work will be a reflection of the Emerald Tablet and that every time it's read something new will be extracted from its pages. Hence I invite you to 'let go' when you read, feel the words, and see the images between the lines. I am recalling a past of which we have forgotten only momentarily.

Listen to what your mind says and then have a dialog with the Universe. This book is freedom for me and I hope for others as well.

Thanking you in advance for listening.

A TarMan Celebrating his Natural Kink.

BOOK I

Speaking 'I AM' in shades of black

It fell into the bronze palms of a copper school child
with microscope knuckles. No one knew but he could
see into the bacteria of souls.

my story

I was 13 clay dolls spread across the Sudan
on the lips of sand storms
yesterday's limbs torn
through tomorrow's futures
ailments that sit on the edge of mani-cures
red and gold bursts of knowledge
traveled through pressed fingerprints
on the wings of globalization

It can be told behind the cries of babies
sneaking out of their screams
between gasps of air
in the fourth break beat of folk songs
walking through distilled quiet
places where words are life
and non-verbal communication
spark silent poems with loud messages
Can you hear me now ?

My story has no strings attached
dangling live bait at this man eat man existence
it has looked through policemen with cross eyes
purchased enlightenment
from store brands on New Years
returned brain washed genes on Easter
I am nothing more than who I claim to be
shaped by some, molded by others
soaked in the experiences of ancestors
traveling through the shape of mouths
the length of necks

It is of ocean's tongues
discernable from 20,000 feet above heaven
tangled in a recipe of disaster eaten by gods
who play life with pawns birthed in human thought
It belongs to my mother
she uses it to beat cassava
and stretch pepper pot soup
across weeks of $6 per hour
My story went to sleep one night and woke up
as a reason to live.

flesh.soul.intact

Stay with me
till I can float you
on the winks of rain clouds
pupil my understanding of why
you are here
next to me
sing me waterfalls
98% is liquid in your hands
seal your palms
to stay in touch
the length of your life lines
prophesized that your future
is with me
let me
sleep wrinkles
knuckles
tight fists
grinding
womanhood into
Girl
Baby
Embryo
Ovaries
Egg
Sperm
I met your eye lashes
open to me
33 years ago
slow
low
blood pressure
retinas adjusting the whole of me
on my way to being born
on my way to finding
God in me
I found you in God

So if it's my soul you want then take it
but leave my flesh intact

Leave tangibles I can hold
my soul can find its way back
it breadcrumb my shadows
but as for you
I lay in your conversation
like hellos
like your breath in halos
familiar as your face
as your fading view
of me
left longing
focused in your dreams

I dreamt you lost
in moments green which
reserve my flesh
hold you a space
on an empty bench
in the bite of winter
shadows of clock towers
and music
there's music there
floating the wind
syncopation timing your love
momentarily
lost in tunnels
brought back on
voices that follow bus routes
toward higher learning
toward ambition
abroad countries
a broad plane
off kilter
nonsensical
but divine

It doesn't make sense to you
but this song is sung in your pitch
you knew its tempo
the first time you believed
possibility
the death of alone
the moment you smelled it

barefooted
breathing in the sun
breathing in stardust

I swam through 12 midnights
half past last conversations in double talk
the sound of my name
move past your lips
hips shifted
ego inverted
so I love only me in your smiles

Who am I
this Jack of all trades
with typhoon pressed dreams
against your skin
rubbing the imprint of your desires
into flesh
like rice paper
like ice makes up my heart
I wish for you to find
what you are searching for in his DNA
but everyday
I fall back in love with you
every five minutes
every time I shed skin
every time I make room to swallow

want to build solar panels in your pupils
so you can see me pure energy
pure light
true
mimic your blood type
cure you a dream

Homeopathic telegram me
into a migraine
saliva filled vowels
pronounce your orgasms
in the hard sounds of consonants
my consequence
measures your secretions
in grams of fat

wait watchers
of the journey will skinny dip
your illusion into a gallery
into a book of flames
into the yolk of an elephants heartbeat
into empty mornings dipped in velvet tea
glued shut with jam and marmalade
into the story of my life
into my flesh colored off white
with a chocolate throw
so you know
that if its my soul you want
then take it

but leave my flesh
to cry the imprint your hands made
when you last touched me
beautiful

Patois

De wey se you gwan
mek mi whan tek off
all a di foolishness
dat mi mek up hide
unda neat mi skin

What is this thing
that hangs in the lining of my throat
underneath it all
that after taste left
on my fingers once I
call your bluff

Nuff respect fi di people dem
tek time darling
no need fi hurry
err ting cook and curry
but wait.....Bomba
who eva tek up mi heart string
betta bring it back
soon
seen
You in the distance
pixilated ashes of a left over flame
picturesque beauty
with a Dorian gray emblem
carved into the corner
slightly out of sight

Las night
 dopey tek wey
 mi dreams
and dash dem wey
dis morning
I one wake to find
 dem between unu fingas

I figure you belong to my future
cause I keep trying to sleep you into yesterday

i am

Last night I swallowed mirrors
fell asleep looking for
a new view of myself
woke up to an odd image
an image of the President
hustling the Pope for the Underground
blue prints of the Ghetto
Mona Lisa blowing in his hands
for good luck
Condoleezza up his sleeve
I heard him whisper
"red top raises make blacks fold by the 1000's"
he said
I raise you society
poured into a Petri dish
filtered through microscopes
we've held them between church and state
and now that we control their money
we need to constitute their faith

My view of me to date
has been altered on an atomic level
since the days of sand rain
between Tuskegee experiments
making clay dolls
with images on Nefilim[1] dictators
dictators dictating creation
from standstill dreams
they stretched me recreated
chromosomes published
"connect the dot" slave ship manuals
for easy replication
advertised free National Geographic
head shots in VIBE and XXL
but now I have doubled X'd
and appear to you as cloned black man
kalimba capillaries fed by CNN

---

[1] The Ancient Secret of the Flower of Life. Vol 1, page 84

drum beats in my heart
hollowed echoes reverberating
Claude McKay
Stokley
Countee Cullen
Mohammed
Mustafa
Walker
Ali
GK Osei
Okri
Yusef
Tubman
CLR James Baldwin
Nathaniel
Hannibal
Giovanni
Osiris
Isis
Tshaka,
Menelik
Imhotep today
you tomorrow
yesterday we were Philistine

I am revolution brushed with Dogon
20/20 Sirius B vision[2]
walking down a famished Broadway block
using Mondrian street map
codes to hack into Disneyland
they've been slipping us mickeys
tight rope around my neck
tomorrow in a sling
sorting through sugar cane sweat
record labels to define my ingredients

I played BET
on Nintendo game boys worldwide
they've gamed black boys
in the world while, MTV tutors

---

[2] The Ancient Secret of the Flower of Life. Vol 1, page 13

held handcuffed kindergarten classes
in their mouths.

I found the word PEPSI
in MS WORD spell check
best believe NIGGAZ will be
spelled out in version 10.0
I am cloned Negro
Africa in my veins
carrying my nigga name embossed
American Express black card
member Since 1804.
they forced me to leave home without it

I am the usual suspect
with a permanent limp
crip walking with shackles
a staving vegetarian in a herd of buffalo
I can only be as I am told
even when I am told I am not
wrestling with demons that resemble progress
I am a Brooklyn slave
inside a crack pipe
in the middle of a poppy seed
in Afghanistan picking cotton
with blank panthers at my heels
black Jacobins on my birth certificate
using Malcolm X postage stamps
to shop at Target
bull's eye tattooed
to black boy mosquitoes
'these bloodsuckers think
I can't feel them bite'

I am America's handprint
on Hutu machetes
wearing mud cloth blindfolds
and cotton fields stuffed in my ears to
muffle the sound of severed generations.
I see the moons orbit in metaphors
ready for the world
armed with cliff note heritage
a Jamaican terrorist plot

to recapture reggae music
rewind selector cuz Babylon soon come

I am 'New Brand' Negro
brand New Negro
franchise Negro
with Nike Chakras included
preloaded ice grills sold separately
at conflict with conflict diamonds
creating conflict
around heroes being made outta
pimps and convicts

I am chicken bones in a Gunnie sack
thrown into clouds to distinguish our future

I am the stakes
for the Pope and the President
till I realize what's really at stake
for the Pope and the President

I am a black man
at the age of confusion
looking for a new view of myself.

our daughters' immune

I have read about her

squeezed tears
from newsprint sorrows
her images hyphenate the fours letters
between death
disease comes in 31 flavors in her world
mud huts harbor patriarchal
traditions that feed the soul but
destroy the heart
the flies.
lord knows
the flies carry her identity
seen through 10000 eyes at once
casting multiple views
blurring her truth

She is dark
rich
driven like molten lava
cooled by the breath of gods
limbs carpentered by pain
eyes shaped by hashed wind
blackened from its burn

Her spirit
bottled for future use
sold to whomever
seems to care for the moment
she smiles from inside
preserving her strength
offering surface grins
as solace to her little siblings
we call her Malawi
daughter of Namibia
granddaughter of Saharan Africa

Her body is only thirteen years

30 pounds in weight
30 million forgotten dates
wrapped around her waist
but she's lost 80000 pounds
since I saw her last year
ravaged by hunger
her appetite stolen
by acquired immunity
deficiency
dictates her dreams
her screams muffled by tribal laws
her babies' invisible
lifeline divisible by the triumphs of
her husband's plights
but since his death
her existence left to be
reborn in the arms of spouses' relatives
incest carved within the blueprints of folklore

She is defined by disease
her life has punctuated
the fours letters between death
A - Malawi **I** - Namibia **D** - Southern Africa **S**

ghetto hope

Amidst the shanty towns and
unpaved streets of colored America
thrives the cornhusk fed presence
of communal abstinence

Amidst the crowed alley ways and
dusty stairwells of colored America
thrive the stench of broken down work-boots
strewn across makeshift
clotheslines casting shadows
on rolled up condoms
fresh from post sex emancipation
ten-dollar crack head gratification

Amidst the barrios of the #1 local
the Ghettos of colored America
oozes the contaminated
shrieks of un-fed children
cared for by un-wed children
longing for their monthly
satisfactions from
pre-fabricated bank checks
of an un-just government

Yet out of these perfectly surviving worlds
breathing in effortless
from their own innate
mixture of sullen experiences
alcoholic drenched existences
forever idle in their safe place
content in this circular life
hovers the nocturnal rustling of hope
And it sways with the most
insignificant of whispers
back and forth between
the trashcans and
urine stained basements
as if singing some gentile lullaby
so thick that it clings madly to the thoughts
of those that recognize its glimmer

messenger

If I placed you
in a glass jar
blackened the outside
with charcoal
took you to the ends
of the galaxy
and let you float
on your dreams

Your intensity
would
sparkle
so bright
that you
would
alchemy
diamond
memories
back to earth
so that
I could
breathe
you in
stardust

insects at sunrise

Last moon
I sent a letter to GOD
it came back marked
return to sender
so I am still waiting
for an answer from the heavens
about what this all means.
this morning I woke up groggy
found an image perched
on the corner of my bed
and as I cleared my senses
I realized that it was a figure of a woman
with a dolphin head

her panted breath
moved in odd patterns
1 2 breathe
4 5 6 breathe
8:00 in the morning don't bode well
so in a drunken sleep state I bellow out
"who in the fuck are you"

You called me here she said
so here I am
floating on the eyes of June
and I've been watching you
since you played in Giza sandcastles
before then even
when Atlantians drew your image
in the petals of life
so your fire would live on forever
and after 3 cycles you remember
remember, we are twin souls
light energy split
 we descended into Hell's fury
reborn in amnesia's fetal
positions Illumination carved
to our heads squinting
chakras shocked into 1/3 pulse rates

we spaced each other in millenniums
I ran with Hermes
you with Gilgamesh
I saw you once with Jason
tried to sing you away
but you recognized my siren
calling you closer to demise
I never forgot you
21 years into my third return
GOD whispered your axis

You called me here
to rejoin flames
ignite the invisible
lines that connect
female to the planes of time
to touch the inner most
flower that protects pollen
from the ideal of escaping
into the intoxicating lure of air
see this here
is for us
insect survival

Food to flower flowers
we can carry twenty times
our emotional weight
we build life inside
Gulliver's footsteps
those beyond our level of sight
have already walked this path
larger than us but part of us
we have grown 4 more chromosomes
we communicate through skin
collecting memories
that have yet to be shaped

I am here and you beckoned me
do you remember who I am ?
can you recall the time we danced as light
climbed through black holes
skipped galaxies
where infinity is an ideal

that seems to go on forever
But you and I realized that it was the circle of time
simply repeating itself in different dimensions
so its familiarity was lost to the rest of existence

Don't you remember?

I am not your reflection
but the source
I am you
until you remember me
you will never find yourself

I am here
you are here
in the heavens
addressing your own letters
sending secret messages to yourself
hoping that you will
read away your amnesia

eardrums

Listen to the hiss of snake children
spitting razor blades
the profound flavor of profanity
grasping at their taste buds

Logos burned in their skulls
from fitted caps
a new era
a Brooklyn bomber
dipped in bleach
their 9MM attached corneas
shooting for street cred
folding ignorance into rock star monologues
Garvisms embossed under their skin
dissolved into their bone marrow
for safe keeping
marked in body tattoos
for safe keeping
inking their lost identity in their veins
for safe keeping
marked in zoot suit blackface
for safe keeping
marked in sagging pants
combing locks into a konk flavored fantasy
draped in platinum shackles

These brooding packs of wingless dreams
floating kicks
floating graffittied jeans
their feet competing colored pastels
relaying races
in telepathic head nods
'I exist' bent into hand signs
'I am here' spent seeking approval
from fathers with sir names embroidered in
the aerodynamics of their absence
catching the fleeting swoosh of
concentration camps in their eyes
in their bar-coded skin

We have bought their allegiance
with technology
with gilded promises
speaking inverted slang
speaking venom
spitting a language
mutated into the uncultivated
spasms of liquid school girls
drunk with the dripping stench
of strip bars
magnetic strip bar codes
sell their wombs to preserve virginity
tutoring their mannerisms
in pole hieroglyphics
the Rosetta stone in their pupils
translated by the ringing
of angel wings
these Angels sing in 3rd speak
the antebellum of sanity
forget me knots
in the belly of their branded wombs
call me arch angel
remember my name divine
weave me into silk
spin me unconscious
they are
the wanting waiting
the crust scrapped from the
eardrums of humanity
their tucked in jeans
their belted demure
refusing to give their
vaginas a place to escape
these are our children
their Eardrums stretched
deaf to the mega hertz
of love,
these are of children
eardrums stretched
death from the mega hurts
of the voice patterns of our lies
These
Our Children

alchemy

I pucker balance
between views
of your laughter
in sleep
while daydreaming
of ashes
highlighting the yellows
of you

I am
pregnant
with your scars
they are self inflicted
I feel the tight
in my neck
whenever your blood
kisses air

I wear your pain in lifelines
closed and raised high
above my shoulders
alchemy
thrust into infinity

Like a black magician
discovering
his halo
still intact

BOOK II

In the Beginning

In the beginning you placed your hand in the mouth of a soothsayer brushed against his wisdom tooth. You would have pricked yourself had he not forewarned you but the path of natural occurrence made a drop of blood trickle from your fingertip since it was meant to happen anyway. It fell into the bronze palm of a copper school child with Microscope knuckles, no one knew but he could see into the bacteria of souls when he clenched his fists and held it high in defiance of the vacant lots of his desire and Alzheimer memories. When focused, he noticed within the blood, Africans sewing Kente cloths together to cover his DNA strands. Confused as to what he witnessed, he cut himself forming a scab that he could pick communication from. They were frightened of blue-eyed caterpillars cocooned in the hills of the Caucus mountains. They stole into the night to steal their destinies, during their yearly hunt for freedom blossoms. It had been that way for four millenniums now.

These vixens of reflection, lured by the taste for civilization before civil was even defined as a nation. Seems these caterpillars were in awe of their speaking in bronzed sunrises and orange moons. They were enraged by the way they danced the moonlight of harvest. Umkosi[3] stabbed jubilation with kinetic smiles. They survived with their wombs in the middle of liquid ocean of gold. The child's eyes grew weary as these pillars of wonder talked to his pupils and allowed him to see through their memories and spread the tale of their demise. In the camouflage of half sleep echoes, they hid in a Chiwara[4] horns, using the intricate make up of its body language to attract eyes, even the third ones lay hard-pressed on this interment. Damned, these parasites of parasites infested with green-eyed termites lived for 23 minutes; their wooden hearts eaten during the maturation process. Those that survived, emerged from cocoons as butterflies with metal wings that reflect the sun and burned holes in the outer skin of blood drops where these Africans lay. With fierce dedication they wanted to destroy the first man. They sort to resort to untamed barbarian Viking like tactics. Warring parties with flags that donned names from Thor to Plato, Horus to Nato, Socrates and Sophocles, they

---

3 Zulu name for the 'first-fruits' ceremony, held annually.

4 Mythical antelope of Mali symbolizing harmony between men and women

were in a sorority of numbers. They worked to replace our honey suckle sap dreams with rancid milk squeezed from their thorax, nestled in the ridges of a pink abdomen and shriveled breasts. In the midst of a prayer, the Africans called out split tongue to the heavens and asked for the hearts of a thousand legends and the innocence of a school child. I whispered in their ear what my mother's Orisha wanted them to do. They covered their DNA Strands to detract the appeal, leaving caterpillars circling around their own actions. Forced to develop cold dances that make clank sounds when wings were brought together.

In the midst of their gloating, caught in the delight of themselves, they forgot for a moment the shuttle plays of the African stance. The bold strokes of its movements and strength. They forgot the orange moons of the Africans and that the sands of instance slide down mountains like liquid glass in the hours of time since the beginning of time which they saved in the barks of willow trees for cooper school children like me. In this drunken stupor, encased in a shell of shear self- love it was easy to catch them. To catch a nectar-ing butterfly, you come up from the lower backside of humanity concluding your thoughts as you pass their bodies in one easy motion. Ignorant for years they don't see your imagination as easy as they do bullets piercing clouds. The sound commonly made when you pick them up with thumb and finger. He covered their abdomens with Kente cloth made of eleven pieces of skin from the backs of fathers to suffocate their evil. Before they could recover, they were made to lay in want, before they knew that yearning existed. Unable to breathe and without food their feelings became numb, thoughts sparked electric messages through their stomachs and across their wings. But the connections were no longer made. Their molecules no longer hold weight in the mass of existence. They were dying. Dying to take what was ours. Determined in numbers to steal our DNA strands that are coupled with the knowledge of forgotten lands.

So my friends, as I look into the bacteria of souls with my clenched fists held high in defiance of my vacant lots of desire and Alzheimer memories. Should you happen to nick, slash or bleed, be watchful of where your blood drops fall. For there are those out there who will walk in triangular paths to swallow your DNA and orgasm in the mouth of a soothsayer. Makes you wonder; would you have gotten cut in the first place had you not put your hand in and tried to see the future.

BOOK III

Recognized Strangers

I only wanna feel you from the inside

chapters

When reptiles bubble into the beginning of
sunrise smiles
I awaken to the smell of you
bright and burning ethers
swirling Merkaba with mint green glows
but I am still here lifeless
riding the shadows of prophecies casted by the walls
Jerusalem left behind
you are burned into chapters
my history cannot tell

Part One

I have planted your placenta under a sycamore tree
and returned for food only
laced latex memories over your distance traveled
cause I can't catch what you got
the weights on my ankles won't allow me to reach your light
so I read the writings on the walls you left behind
incorrectly
my perspective is warped from this angle
and I can't make you out from here
can't make you up for fear
and don't know if I should love you
or come back when your fruit blooms
seeds I can spread to other baron lands
this is not about you
but about the acorn life I've traveled
from falling branches …..hitting rolling stones
papa was……..

Part Two

Papa I hear you in my throat when I inhale
think about your coarse hands but gentle touch
and how Jamaica fed you volcanoes
and you left hurricanes for me to tame
I am forged with the blood of your conviction
but temptations have taken over my hands
and when I grab a hold of fidelities shadow

I can taste the stench of you in my movements
press forward I recognize you
move backwards I recognize you
grab hold I recognize you
remember the secrets that built dams
in my memories of why she wasn't
the one who made you smile like that....seems
frowns have painted their impression of you
into her paint strokes
on the days when
mama said

Part Three

Mama said there be days like this
where scattered logic will stumble upon your cries
and you will sweep your questions into a mound of
fabled vaginas wet from the dew of bright light mornings
but if you access my axis
she said
you will find that my spine is locked to your locks tight
right side mirages
left side thoughts of pubescent cheeks
that suckle yesterday sins into grown men
looking for who we were to them then...
in their eyes
then
in their tears
then
but not you my child
cause I have laid
humble at your tongue and fire in your belly
so go forth and burn presumptions in the
teeth of the clenched masses
trust your kisses
cattle your experiences into forever steps
and collide with the faint at heart
your grand mothers start their days battling the demons
you can't see
see
these chapters
know your jargon

speak your flavor
and protect your skin
from the sun like
reptiles bathing in the warm abyss of sunstrokes
able to convert heat into cool
so…
begin each day under the shroud of
sunrise smiles my son and

I too will awaken to the smell of you

Part Four

I am here even when you feel alone

he

If I am of earth
you are my water
I can feel you covering the most of me
giving life to baron regions where hope
has buried itself beyond the reach of rain fall
you are making the universe spark magma
visions that burn away the shell
I have grown accustomed to
I am naked out here now

Wanting to be free
knowing that this feeling
is not widely accepted
that when destinies
have been etched in granite
the only way to change them
is to the destroy that which wrote it
baby I've studied the future
already know that it's coming

Been trying instead to
circle myself in the silence of my demands
when demands are silent
who can hear them

If I stare determined
into the dense patterns of life
will something
someone notice
that we are stars
with extension cords
shining faster than sound
giving light to the faces of want
before the sound of impossible
in this lifetime
can be heard

Burn through my expectations
make my absolutes
watery spells of thirst
lingering in the bottom of oceans

with no light
where creatures survive in the dark
communication is touch
togetherness formed through vibrations

Muse me

Like you have done for centuries
when we lived as animals
protect each other from the perils of existence
evolution never seep between our grasps
we are as we were
before all of this
we could hold each other
in one way
focused within
cyclops sights
dedicated to what makes the earth turn

It's been a long time coming
and change gon' come
let it come around us
but not between us
because if you shade memories
on the face of a blank page
you can always see the impression
of what was written in the past

i want to

Make love to you in final ways
my face buried in your neck
hands somewhere above your thighs
your eyes searching mine
while we drive
quietly

I want to
make love to you with your knees
between mine...fully clothed
but thinking about it

I want to
be inside of you when
I am alone and doing other things
with my hands going placidly unnoticed

I want to
touch your lips and
weave the shape of you
then with the form of you now
whisper things reminiscent
ancient belonging only to us

I want to
be with you recreating
shifting from belly things
to something flying
capturing us in endless
miniscule moments
moving

In and out with time
I want to make you
mine

ruby brown (circa 1997)
inspired by L. Hughes

She was young and beautiful
sweet like natures own creation
golden like the sunshine
that warms her body
she was black
Manhattan
had no place to offer her
no solitude no love
nor momentum
to ignite the spirit
within her soul
matter of fact
one day sitting
on her broken own fire escape
outside her one room tenement
overlooking Saint Nicholas
soaking her feet in hot water
and Epsom salt
she asked herself two questions
they muttered through her
sweet breath
as she shuddered
what can an Afro American woman do
on the money from cleaning
a white woman's kitchen
fetching her children from school?
and ain't there any joy in this town
of bright lights?

At night
the street lights
overlooking Saint Nicholas
know more about this
pretty Ruby Brown
the dark dank alleys
hold a brown girl
searching for answers
to her two questions.

The good church folk

of Agnus Baptist
do not call her name no more
no more that ol' Ruby Brown
be working her fingers to the bone.
but the white men
occasional habitants
of those damp alleys
pay more money to her now
than they ever did before
when she worked in their kitchens
for services rendered
sharpened steel tendered
through thick skin
answers all the questions
posed by pretty Ruby Brown

That ole Ruby Brown
be working her fingers to the bone
when she's finished work
she'll drag her weary body home

Pretty Ruby Brown

letter to my unborn son

Son

This is an urgent message
tied to a piece of me fractured into
images of you as a God whisper

You are sapped from the nectar of
artisans and tribesmen alike
but you already know this
your ancestors have already shaped
your genetic code
so this is not about that
not about how much you will amount in life
but whose life you will amount to be

This is an urgent message
written on the skin of lust
edited with a kiss
hidden on the tail ends of a single sperm cell
to encode your DNA with the
single most
important warning
before you're born

Don't follow your father footsteps

sent to you by way of the uterus
because far too many of us
have orgasmed into adulthood
with flamed fists finding light at the end
of enslaved wombs

I want more for you

This is about love before survival before
fallopian secretions vasectomy your heart
Stone
before my bad habits
corrupt the surface of your mother's belly
Metal

before you recognize disappointment in my voice
Disdain
before my voice
Invisible
my voice
Cold

before your tears clone hate
my mistakes have vacuumed
the tails of sperm secrets in far too many
have stolen wombs only to have them reborn
in little girls
who could have carved
my eyes into generations

Son, this is about love

About holding its forever insanity on the roof of your mouth
so as to taste it in every word spoken
and I've have loved in place where light and dark are strangers
at a time when my tears were integers of her smiles
evenly spaced lullabies looking
so far into the abyss
that I couldn't see her love as endless
and even though I proved her's finite
I have burrows her name into
my past as the woman who isn't was
and coffined her soul because
soul mates come in flavors
so capture love wild
in human zoos
in paper machete
with honey on your fingers
ball your fist in defense of a kiss
explain nothing
feel everything
but love in quiet
cause your future
cant be responsible with relationships
it's already looking for the next moment
so be present to her now

Your heart can't do

what you eyes can't see
so grow sight in your veins

The square root of your happiness
will be in her touch
raw, naked
sung in a headlock
the size of tornadoes dancing

Use the echo of your
bodies rubbing together
to vibrate this earth
from sleepwalking genesis
always undress your ego
and you will watch conceit go blind

I pray that this finds
you waiting
embryo inhaling memory
as this maybe the last chance to pass
on this caution
abortions have already
cattled the names of your siblings
before I could caveat their deliveries
so see me
earnest
before you see me flesh
forgive me
urgent
before my sperm enters egg
and you enter existence
as a God whisper
tied to a piece of me
fractured into your image

Remember your father's footsteps
but be sure to change
direction from
time to time

feeling

I can feel
the electric
when you
come
close
static
making the hairs
on my arms
stand at attention

I can feel
the charge
crawling tenaciously
toward the back of my neck
itching
and
clawing its way
around my spine
ticking
within dips
and groves
as it goes
along

I like this feeling

land of the brave

This is where America lies
in the slanted Z's
of civilizations using only O'
to colour life
forgetting all the U's
that made its brilliance remembered

Lost in stripped flower petals
fluttering on the edge of turbulence
peeking through clouds
the thoughts of sunray children
sit on the thread of plastic seats
melting their expectations

It whispers stillborn promises
anchored in the stomachs of
'Good things to come'
layered atop lies that cross rivers
like bridges gabbled roofs
with Spanish tile foyers

Hide knee prints of Jamaican nannies
Peruvian wash women
unclaimed through the bloodstream
of Park Avenue aristocrats
and Washington state
fundraiser mammograms
the matte candor
of red brick floor wax
cover their palm prints making
trump fortunes invisible
behind closed doors
but in the good ones
I can be seen in hand gestures
boardroom presentations
swimming with sharks
is common place
but an escovitch porgy
is golden caviar

America revels in eating
the unborn species
of what it does not identify with
readily

the awful reality is that it is eating itself
from the outside edges in
cause the world as it is told in the stories of unicorns
was spawned from the blowholes of dolphins

America with broken links
seduced by the forbidden lure of Latin roots
and dreams wrapped in toga drapes

Broken into names of Africans
who swam in 1600 fathoms of ocean abyss
shipwrecked levels
left breathing thorough memories of stars
their futures hold sandpaper burns
from the scars of starboard escapes

Fortunately liquid Gods smiled patience
and mated them with starfish for resilience
algae feed with the reds of time corals
and made them accustom to seeing in the darkness

But all of this was happening under the shroud of winter
so this history casts no shadows on it's
redlined shores

So America continues to play with itself
holding hands with denial tucked tightly
knees pressed to chest
so that somersaults
from the heights of arrogance
do not brush those that await its plunge

Yet we try to grab hold in mid-flight
severing arms
leaving us unable to grasp our own destinies
having to rely on the gust of wind left behind
to guide our children's paths

The skies are at your feet in America
and the glass ceilings have footprints
parents are cloned in America
and the doted lines on maps
that divided continents have moved
cause all the while
they were hibernating ants
sleeping in warring formations
awoken by the shift in the equator

And it's lighter on this side of the world
it's indigenous folk invisible to each other
but bubbling in the mixture of carbonated blood stains
tickling the nose of other countries
writing their smell in history books
but leaving no pictures

'America was here'
but no one saw them come through the front door
they travel through the midst of spray paint
on the ends of hair clippings
between the hard sounds of consonants

America is eating itself
from the outside edges in
and inviting the rest of the world
to join him at the dinner table

subtitles

Love has shortened my arms
leaving me reaching for
transparent gains and taupe colored memories
glued back together with recycled memoirs

My weeps are losing ground
in snarls and knots of
gastric juice and bile
churning in the belly of love
parting the air silently and
meddling in the attention span of pictures
with unrecognized faces smiling back at me

I remember that she had
red caterpillar eyebrows and volcanic skin
she spoke in fireplace embers
as if she had released
hot wax stored in the cheeks
of senile grandmothers
who read bedtimes stories to her at night

Reservoirs of words
she traveled with rubber boots
as her footsteps were electric
carbohydrate energy siphoned from overweight
gluttons and dyslexic anorexics
she was fat with pain
gorged and untamed

Ya see
I was dying at first
I was bright red and spoke in subtitles

My need for her understood by a few
and even then
only selections from
unrehearsed patrimonies

I felt her in the morning
a sound in my ear at first

and then like spilled milk
over the last page of a novel
melted into obscurity
leaving a marked stain
on my comprehension of
tempered outcomes

My desires for her were
hidden in a Trojan horse
made of thousand wooden spiders
that shared only three eyes
manifested in chapters

Chapter one:
Inoculated passion budding from the blossoms of incipient prophets

Chapter two:
Fetishes entangled in petrified ambivalence with
historical fiction passed around at will

Chapter three:
Angels dodging snowflakes for fear of weighted promise
with wings encircling my body encasing me in the midst of ice
crystals that smelled of blueberries

I loved the fear of loving her

days like this

Mama said there'd be days like this
there'd be days like this
my mama said

But she never said that it would feel quite like this
that it should burn sulfur from
the friction of our movements
never have slight shifts in single degrees caused
such apocalyptic waterfalls of electric bonfires
voltage meter spikes
sea Kelp seedlings breaking through ocean floors
crocodile gargles
fathoms deep in the yolk of lust

Never knew the blues could be played
with heated hip grinds and the stench of my
baptism incisions drowned by your tickled
ivory fingernails scaring erratic
Adinkra symbols
on my back

Mama never said

She never said that you would have Orisahs
pausing in mid flight trying to digest your sparkle
voodoo priestesses making Dorian Gray dolls from
watercolors sapped from my soul's landscape
and once…
once
I even dreamt of a Rabbi performing Bris
at a bar mitzvah
while being served
brisk
within the whisper
of a Brisk Autumn breeze
in July
holding Shiva under their coats
see the death of my innocence is apparent

and most of this shit don't make sense to me
but I am a student of the ages
and never to old to learn

So learn me

Learn me
the proper way to squeeze the pulp of your
hibiscus kiwi between my thumb and forefinger
help me to understand Rosemary hues
around the crevice of your back spasms
saffron sprinkles
poisoned gaps
honey flavored
cunnilingus purple intersection
juxtaposed with frenzied un-doings
peeking through the sides of lace thongs

Learn me
how to color close to the silhouette of your
nonsensical speech patterns after the
thrust of eighth notes in 4:4 time
as we finger my name in the puddle of our
DNA leftovers
till the M E's and U's hydrate together
into wets spots
on my side

Teach me how to chew on your climax

Describe for me the process
of how to lather your hips
across my thighs and
the ways in which you can swallow
me whole…cause
I only wanna feel you from the inside

I need to saturate my gums
setting my tongue to convulse labia twitches
I need to smooth out the welts made on the underbelly
of my scrotum when you whisper messages

in the greasy sections of sex
that I don't find till days after
in public spaces
late night snacks
backdoor entries

Through exaggerated glances
I can see the wiggle back-speak of your legs
that fleshy trunk of your calf that shakes
in two or more times
depending on the impact of my pounding

I sing slave songs in between those vibrations
cry freedom after each elastic recoil
shackled to this moment
these solitary trappings have us
rubbing bodies vigorously
till our mouths become ashy
our skin bubbles pinecone ripples
the size of cantaloupes

Learn me your movements

Dictate the dichotomy of dangling
delusions digging directly toward
my deepening metaphor deposits

Mama said there'd be days
but she never said anything about this.

BOOK IV

Lenny Speaks

Lenny Williams croons from an old boom box seated gingerly against the mantle piece. The fireplace below hasn't worked since they moved in and this winter is colder than any this decade. One of those Chicago winters just cold like nature is all pissed off at the human race.

(music) You know I love you. It got so bad that I thought I would roll up in a big ole ball and die.

"Damn" feels like Lenny is talking straight from my stomach.

(music) You know I love you .

I mouth the words to her silently. My breath freezes in the cold and floats across the room to her eyes tight and lips pressed. I can see a smile sneaking its way out between her chattering teeth. And me I'm feeling ashamed at the position I've put her in. Ashamed at the promises of the world of the money the house the cars but she doesn't have any of it; except this broken mantle piece and old cassette tape that's been played thin.

(music) I got dreams…………I got dreams to remember

Well she recognizes the effort he makes. The way he helps out around the house when she put in extra hours. The way he says from time to time that the food tastes good. The cassette tape he keeps in the top drawer behind the handkerchiefs he never uses. It was music that brought them together. The rhythms that represented what they were that later became something unrecognizable. The sounds that were created by someone else that they expected would someday give them the inspiration to be who they really were meant to be if it had not been for the cold. The whistling frigid cold that crept between cracks that weren't fit for caulking. Besides it's a fire hazard how would they get out ?

Nature was angry with them as far as she was concerned. What thing in nature gets together because of something as foolish as

Lenny Williams? There's got to be feathers with a certain extra color not like any other or a voice that sounds above anybody else's. Then there was the issue of protection. But it was Lenny that kept things tight like mud between straw and large wooden beams. Because of Lenny it was dry at the very least.

What else would anyone need but good music he thought to himself watching her squirm around in her seat the way she used to when you asked her something she didn't really feel comfortable answering like when they first met. Funny thing is that it was a gig that he wasn't too excited about playing.

The club manager was one of them wanna be Negro mafia cats with New York City connections always ready to cheat someone outta their deserved pay. But that night none of that mattered. He sat on a small wooden stool sweating from the stage lights. About to start on his second set when he noticed her by the bar smiling at the bartender and giving off that 'open body' language that his high yellow cousin Bernard him taught him 'bout in their junior college classes they was taking. Bernard always knew a little something about a lot of nothing in particular. He played for her that night. Notes wrapping around her neck. Eighth notes crawling down her thighs quarter notes brushing against her breasts. The song was in 4:4 time but seemed like it lasted forever. Sound hesitating jumping back and darting forward keeping her looking guessing feeling keeping her focused. He played for her that night like she was the only one that could hear.

She knew he was looking at her but she played it off just like her mama taught her to. "Don't no man want no woman chasin' him" she use to say. So she chased someone else. Someone she knew she didn't want just so she'd have enough space in her life for him. She already knew that even though she didn't yet know him. So she sat close enough to him so he wouldn't have to squint but far enough away for him to have to maneuver the crowd, if he wanted to talk to her bad enough that is. He would have to do that at least to get through the front door. To the average girl he might not have been much to look at but she was a queen. To a queen he was royalty. His hands looked as though they had been carved from wood sanded and polished to look as smooth as glass. His eyes were so deep they appeared to open when they finally talked. She would have chased him if her mama would have let her. And he could turn your head. In fact if you were not distracted you would be inclined to stare and in her own brand of staring she realized he was a man who had something that he might not share with everybody but for her he would find a way. "Find a way to communicate with her" he thought while cleaning his mouthpiece. He wiped the condensation of the side of his trumpet deliberately enough so that he could see her reflection behind him. She was looking squinting almost trying to anticipate his next move. "Granddaddy used to say we players could smell the scent of pussy through a brick wall. "Humph" Baba with his ole' ass; that's why mama poured hot chicken grease on his hands for touching things that he had no business touching. But this here this here was different. He could feel her looking through and around him. He could feel her touching him all over rubbing under the skin to the muscles. He turned around coy-like looking at a spot above her head so it seemed like he wasn't looking when he was. He could see the back of her neck through the mirror behind the bar. Her neck long and bronze her hair curling up in little circles at the nape where the back starts and the neck stops. He caught a glimpse of a drop of sweat rolling down from under her hat. He knew that it was now or never so he gathered himself adjusted his hat to the side so that the brim covered the left eye and gave her the "walk to".. The same "walk to" his daddy taught him and his daddy before that and so on. 'That's how we players walk' daddy would say "like a blues song hanging of the end of a page. "Walk good now brother walk-on" he thought to himself.

Well he looked just like a fool! Walking like he had lost the bottom of his shoe. But he was cool though….real cool "at least he was walking" she thought. At least there's something she could count as the effort she was expecting from a man. "It's a shame eyes like that belong to a man" she thought to herself. Now how was she going to handle this situation? A nigga' on her left arm a nigga' on the right she could manage though. She knew exactly what to do. She flipped one leg over the other and shifted to the right. There were other parts of her he hadn't seen. The guy next to her kept right on talking not knowing that her flirtation with another man had already begun. He was like a buzz in her ear a signal that it was time to make a necessary move.

53

He sat down next to her. She wondered if he was going to say something or if he was just going to pretend not to see the smooth roundness created in her calf or the open doorway to her thighs. She let him order a drink. Maybe he could even take a sip or two but much more delaying would make her second guess his intentions……… "Excuse me" he said . " please pass me a napkin".

That was enough. She made a point of looking in his eyes as she slid the tiny napkin over. He smirked like he knew something would happen so she'd have to make him wait. She turned halfway to the buzzing talker who finally asked her to dance "No" she said just audibly "I'll pass". As her first suitor walked away she swirled her drink in her glass waiting for the next move.

Damn he been working all that time and all she's gonna say is "I'll pass." What type of woman is this" he thought as he took off his hat and wiped his brow. Hesitating for a brief second not so long as to miss his opportunity he leaned over to her side watching how her mouth moved about the glass and how her beautiful throat moved gently down her long neck as she swallowed. "Sure is hot in here tonight" he whispered. As soon as it came out of his mouth he knew it was the wrong thing to say. He could kick himself. Remember he thought "like a blues song hanging of the end of a page that's what you need to be damn it." Hot in here shit that could mean hot the music is hot; hot like the spot is jumping which since he just played the set would have him looking like he was smelling his own draws; just conceded. Or even worse she could think hot like you're sweating and it ain't too lady like. Damn I shoulda said something else he thought. Shoulda said how pretty her hands were or how beautifully seated she was; like a butterfly that sits on the edge of a flower brushing it slightly and matching its moves in a summer breeze. Shoulda said he thought shoulda said.

"Sure is". She interrupted his ramblings. "Carolina hot and the music ain't bad neither" she whispered leaning over just slightly. Her voice was like John Coltrane, Miles Davis, Ella and Ellington all had one daughter and breathed their lives into her soul at the same time; she sang. Her voice sang her words moving like fingers atop the ivory-capped stems of his trumpet. This here is music. This here is music to ones that study music and know what good music can do. This type of woman is music!

He was silent for what seem in his mind to be like 10 minutes. The space between his first words and his last was in methodical slow motion. She heard every word though there were few. The way they rolled off his tongue the gesture of his lips and the sway of his drink in hand. There was not one moment that was left unturned in her memory of that space. And the silence held at the end spoke words that no one else could muster. It was the silence that was the proof. Too embarrassed to stare she sat looking at him in her mind, the strength of his hands the color that flashed in his eyes. There was the way he bent his neck slightly to the side. Did he know that she was already wondering about other parts of him? She decided to stay cool. Listen in the silence and take everything in. She tried to take as much of him as she could imagine cause it was in fact unbearably hot.

To be continued...

BOOK V

Staged Identities

How can you continue to play lover to aborted dreams

necrophiliac

Part 1 – Biting Flesh

His father taught him
how to change his skin
maneuver his bones backwards
shifting intentions

Mastered
voice patterns
into ice needles
tearing heart valves
flesh magnetically
translates his eyesight
to puppet tones

They hold his pupils
in their mouths
and he doesn't know
they carry his sermon
in their skins
he doesn't know that
that they have already
tattooed their confidence
in their first born's cries

He speaks in gun powder
has Gods eyes in his stride
and they by-pass heaven to
lay in his temple tongue
the fine print in their
tonsils read
"I have died twice for your love"

He is sleeping with the dead
and pleads innocent
to romancing poison
into their throbbing clits

He is making Oedipus love
to their corpse

touching them with
twenty foot twigs
to play about
their rotting flesh
they hold their breath
till he twilights their
holocausts
and she
well she
has already 3rd world her
self image
and rests her religion on
dreams and promises
promises cosmetic surgery in his whispers
"I will build you worthy of me"
he tells them in telepathic kisses
back to back
face to face
chest to chest
fire bled finger tips
touching them into
boiling bodies

Heart melting
pierces there skulls
with his electric tongue
right brains dissolving all
common senses
but they've all been
common since
"hello"

Part 2 - Tasting Skin

They don't know
believed that lust was the twin to love
Siamesed their identity to his phone calls
her nation lost independence
for the promise of
new lands and empty dances
side stepped her divinity
into a sky less free fall
plunging into blind infinity

Shedding her skin
to leave trails for her sisters
But her sisters dissolve
their warnings in acid swallows
that they learn to
reserve for him alone

He is a clone
a disease
a carrier in secret
immunity sewed to smiles
cuts out repercussion with razor blades
thin line devotion
stomach acid lined
to digest their world
in a single swallow
was given the world to
swallow on a single act of
free love
but love ain't free
when hurt is left
to pay for the cost
of a single moment
when a smile and wink
kill a sprit

And you
you
eater of the flesh
you continue
to make love to zombies
that remind you of your mothers love

Part 3 - Digesting Bones
How can you continue to play lover
to aborted dreams

59

looking for me

They were looking for me

heard them whispering
my capture song under their breath
sewing concrete boxes into my clothing
like the projects fit me
like the smell of copper
chains wear me well

They found me once
still born in the hearts of hope
greeted me in the past tense
asked me to follow them to nowhere
no wear
these precious metals
they'll make you numb
forget your traditions
come get you some
we've laid them away for eternity
to see how quickly you can forget your
temple mysteries

They've been looking for me since then
Searching in blood red of Bermuda echoes

They had me once
they used their
ten finger Texan hold'ems
had them so far into my back
that I sold them my soul
for compensation
not realizing that
that which made me irresistible
in the first place
made me indivisible to this
pale face
invisible to this
cold race
of mechanical men
white angels with clubbed hoofs

reciting their never ending story
in forked tongue cuneiform writing

they hung deja-vu from my ankles
swung cotton gins from my neck
evaporated ancestors by the minute
I cookied my spirit
found freedom living in my palms
shook the devil's hand
and burrowed beneath their noses
to tap into the underground railroad
They've been looking for me since then

Found me in nightmares
pressed on their daughters skin
Like curiosity
tattooed spices in their blood stream
leaving their souls to explain
why their bloodline drips green

my secrets have seen
foreshadows and
walk through walls
fought battles
distilled from moors
sold like cattle
but still evolved
with Ethiopia shaped eyes
They been knocking on all the wrong doors

But they're still looking
Still hanging live bait
with ghetto scents
trying to capture me with familiar
but familiar
doesn't look like here
and the ghetto was left
on the shores of the Congo
in 1620
they've stacked blacks in spaces
16x20 already
And now ages 16 thru 20
are brain dead

and ready
for double cells
16x20
and we steady
think that history is not cyclical
ain't nothing different than before
they are still mystically poor
articulately deconstructing our
divinity from the core

But they're still looking

heard them whispering
my capture song
behind 16 bars
lyrics killer
back beats banging from my whip
throwing money on sisters
we call bitch
In effect putting slave owner faces
back in the same places
that raped the races
since 1706

I drink Sioux and Iroquois raindrops
immune to their small pox
commune through reincarnated messiahs
with names like
Malcolm and Tupac

So keep looking
for that which makes you whole
cause we are
Louisiana and Nairobi
Kokomo and the Nile banks
we are Brazil and Osiris
left messages on papyrus
for one another
so we'll always be
one step ahead of you

You will never find me
but you'll always be looking

not that kinda poet

Two years ago
the shortest distance
between two points was
only 20 kilometers away from you

Now you realize that love
is larger than the length of
your hindsight
and the amount of times you smile
outnumber the times you breathe
his words into your reality
your reality
borders the
nonsense that commitment can promise you
and in real life if I had
the courage to do what
I know is right
well
I would be able
to do be battle with 32 spirits
dressed in black
with their egos wrapped in black
Egyptian cloth at their feet
in the black of night
mixing black magic
in a black cauldron
But I am not that kinda poet

Not the kind that seduces
seconds thoughts with the
sweetness of imperfection
I have lied, have cheated
but work at transforming
these shapes into a home for
my children to call life lessons
and it's alright if you
can't recognize the flesh
hanging from these sentiments
cause the seconds in between
our last conversation spells
I LOVE YOU

as you are
flawed, faltered, unsure
I will chase your shadows away
light at the end of the journey
will hold on to your feet as you ride the wind
with your eyes closed
grounded
I am not that kinda poet

So don't cast me the form of their gestures
don't galvanize me a statue of
their indecent reflections
my eyes spark their own dreams
and it is not my fault if
you planted them a rose
and they grew your secrets into
pollen to share indiscriminately with the wind

I take my baggage by my side
bound to my waist
to a least steady myself
as I reach outstretched arms
for your understanding
understand him
as a figment of your past
a tuning fork for your experience
But get me
under a stand of your convictions.
through the muck and Meyer
steady your self
pace your thoughts
count the blessings on your fingers
cause sometimes
Simple
well simple
Is better than mechanical

so the next time you search for someone to
penmanship your fears into well crafted excuses
remember
I am not that kinda poet

blond locks

behind her
one love sentiments mist her tongue
Africa spelled backwards spilling from her ankles
like her true heritage was stuck between her knees
she wobbled white American
but stood straight in black face

She appeared to be true
brandishing ghetto spirituals
and holding her conscious up with a black pride belt buckle
but this all seemed strange to him
like he couldn't accept that this white girl
couldn't understand his struggle
empathize with his struggle

hell ….She was his struggle

But he was looking for the pathway
to Sai Baba's arch ways
but still stuck in a near-sighted bubble
and the ancients are telling him to
forget the surface areas cause
one can feel the power of the Sun
even though you can't look at its color directly
so get that this topography holds no indication
toward the heights of her demeanor
hold no weight to the strength of character
and he knows but
but it is hard to let go off the comfort of hate
the pocket of warmth that allows him to blame from a distance
use this crutch as stilts towering over how fucked up they've been
to him and his people
like she herself navigated slave ships
that stole his tongue

He has to find a new language
one that doesn't sound like hate
because he is destined for better things

message in a bottle

She is sitting on bruised petal
separating a wish
into a million mosquitoes
with humming bird wings
floating bad habits
between the hairline fractures
of future smiles

She is thirteen now
203 years old then
before her grandmother buried
butterfly pain in her stomach
carried dandelions squeezed
in the jaw line of her rhetoric
turned east to pray
to a mantis with daddy long leg features
who walked on the edges of her laughter
in the twilight of centuries

He turned God backwards
and saw the end of times
in her Genesis
turned his character askew
to live in the Pegasus of her
eyes colored earth
he became her
morphed into 10 years
past her first childhood
he was a girl
with scrapped knees
who read his future in the palms
of domesticated soothsayers
traced the physics of her life lines
and mapped his way back her future
found images of himself in her memories
holding hands with self portraits
webbed in the miniature footsteps
of sibling half tones
playing the keys of the universe as distant stars
seen from the surface of their thighs

galvanized scriptures of
2005 life times

he imaged himself without a past
colorless
secretly walked into her thoughts
to lay with her alchemy wishes
and swallowed the
residue of fallen butterflies
which made him erase
into the festering belly
of mutated words
choking in the thick of clouds
he caught his breath
on the slight of her chamomile

Found himself
15 years forgotten
in an bottle
floating on a ocean
with a note
clipped to a bruised flower
that read
my heart bleeds mosquitoes
and I wish you to find me again
in the moments between
humming bird wings
where my past expectations
are lost in the hairline fractures of
tomorrow

Tomorrow
he awoke
and found her looking
back at him in the mirror
age 35
wet
with a crushed dandelion between
his fingers
and a wish caught
on the damp
of his floating tears.

red bone red as his friends called him. People say it had to do with the way his hair turned red in the summer time. He strutted that morning, strutted round like a peacock happy with himself cause for him pressures were released.

You see, he had found his way to something that warmed him to the very bottom of his soul. Felt like when the sun just bout to burn the morning dew from the faces of leaves. It felt warm to him, as warm as the green grass that sat under the sun all day and stuck him through the soles of his beat up shoes and he felt good. His daddy's ol work hat tilted to one side, walking along the dirt road with the dust kicking up a cloud behind him whistling and singing:

"I was fitin ta catch her early morning in the months of May. Grab her n whisper in her ear one day. Share with her smiling that she bring my way. Gurl I'm fitin to burst wit all I gotta say. Justa burst'n inside wit what I gotta say".

Red was happy and vowed to himself that no matter what he would remember that feeling for life. The thing bout this brown sugar sweet gurl was that whenever Red bone saw her, his heart would fill up with what seemed like big ol' dragon flies; not dem puny butterfly type, these went whooshing round his stomach and sometimes made their way to his throat and his teeth. Well, his teeth would film over dry, his hands would get damp..and worse of all, he felt, that his tongue would haul off and run down to his belly.

"er..er..er..how you doin Ms Lady...seems ah..ah... like its gonna be a right day for turning soil". Turning soil 'what type a sweet talk is that' he asked on the inside cause on the outside he was Red bone red. The thing bout this sweet girl, what got red underneath that come out in the summer is that she coulda come from only one place; seemed like to him at least. He figured that God was lonely one day and fiddling round wit the same stuff he used to make the earth and the heavens with. Seemed like he carved out this figure added a little rock in it to make it firm, added a little sun in it to make it shine, added a little night in it to give that little bit a mystique, then smooth'd it all out and added a little paprika for color. That's Red bone red for ya thinking and walking wishing and singing waiting for the next time dragons go flying.

To be continued……..

68

bloodline

I have been writing this never-ending poem
with invisible ink
finally
scratched the surface of the page
to reveal that I have carved out a
small place in my heart for you
with a rusty knife
allowed it to heal
with jagged edges
and crusted centers so that each time
your memory runs across its touch
you hurt more than me

I still revel in the circumstances
of what was
and what will be
forced past haunts me in the moments
when I am most happy
not at night when my alone can filter the pain
not during the coarse moments of life
when things all look the same
this flashback comes in between hugs
at the height of love making
on the edges of her smile
during morning breakfast
gentle temperaments turn
sunny sides up grey
and a task as simple as eating eggs
reminds me that no mater how you slice it
we willingly eat the souls of the unborn daily

so I guess you were just testing the waters.
seeing how long embryos float till there skins are pierced
and now
well now years later
I prefer long sleeves
cause I will wear you on my arms for life
wishing away the scars
dancing around veins mixed with the sweat of resistance. All the
while wanting to forgive you

but all the while knowing that the devil plays
in the spaces between the lost and insecure
but all the while knowing that hate
in the black of night
soothes me as I mentally scrap your confessions
onto makeshift wrists whose
bloody clasps hold onto my whispers of
You were old enough to know better
You were old enough to tell him NO
And I didn't know what to do
how to say no
how old does a mind have to be
to understand that shared fathers only and mothers removed
shape the meaning of step brother
You fucking
over stepped
Brother

And I gave my silence to you
like you deserved it
hid blame between the pages of the family albums
between your grandfather's
curled picture and my mother's photo
and you don't belong there

I've created the thin lines between love and hate
trying to separate our blood
with razor blade happy faces
using women to surround myself with love
in repetition
cause there's safety in numbers right ?
can lose insecurity in a crowd right ?
WRONG!

How many fucks were just fucks
cause that's all I could give
how many women have met your character
at the end my unfaithful

and now I don't know how to the reach
the contaminated parts of me
can't reach the screams from here

muffle the sound of the rotten
fragments of me
burning through my rage
paving the uncharted road of
how I do life now
I felt the bite of wide eye reverence as a child
now my eyes are wide shut
and I still wonder how to circle
around the courage to tell this story
to recognize that blood however thick
slips through the fingers of the tightest fists.
and I think I have forgiven you
fifty times over
and meant none of them
have found justification for your actions
and believed none of them
have wanted to reconcile my conflicts
through pad and pen
but I can't even figure out how I feel
after so long
It was so long ago
that maybe this is all for no reason
my cause reached its limit

But maybe
this unwritten letter will somehow
catch flight on the wings of guilt
find you at your end of days
and suffocates your last breathe
with remember fucker what you did
remember how your actions have
shaped the lives of all I've touched
You have been inadvertently
tracing my footprints
and honestly
I don't know how
to love you again
but I will
find a way to mix this invisible ink
with visible scars
and figure out a way to
pick forgiveness from the scabs
you left behind.

fairytales

Her dreams spit street stench
orgasms her surrender into
project foyers
collects purple leaves
from bruised trees
her mid section split
to handle the world
she fucks with twice a day
and she doesn't know
that she gave birth to air

she is carrying the weight of the world
under her skin.
distance traveled in her eyes
and she ain't even
traveled outside her soul yet
ain't gone nowhere but here
but here
gives way to lost dreams
and baby figurines
figures what she seen in life
is colored green
accepts her pain and strive
cause this is how its always been
she's left empty
from open seams
and only sees
rag doll faces
and empty dreams
boy's worn insecurities
boy torn melodies

and she trying to run from them
trying to escape this place
trying to travel to far away places

she just wants to go to far away places
so she sleep walks fairytales
where fish grow gills
in her last name

somersault wind through water
shifting in moments
meant for just her
and just like her
they waterfall stars
and despite the noise
history has left in her head
she caresses silence
like an atomic blast in an kiss
addressed to her unborn daughter
I will be here for you tomorrow
I promise
She tells her
I will grow a mountain in my eyes
to climb your tears
so you don't have to wing your feet
like your mother
don't have to lay naked with secrets

you my child will cut angel wings
from the scars I left freckled in smoke trails

follow my spirit
not my footprints
tie my dreams to gravity
cause even in my fairy tales
I can see gold and green futures
at my finger tips
but can't understand how these
street stench spit dreams
can distance flesh so far
from reality

she is a blue flame
carrying centuries in her breath
an echo collecting healing from far away places
but thinks she needs to search
for what is already there

america

The tears of widowed mothers
quicksand desert secrets
White house sandcastles are being
built by children infected with college bound
who Bleed ROTC from their veins
The president's off switch has malfunctioned
An oil slick the size of national cemeteries

Have you seen the tombstones lately
they read in plural
yet our mothers are complaining that they are
deafened by the unbalanced quiet of single bunk beds
yet
they twice
sleep walked him back in office
how better to stuff the ballot
than with the body counts
Are you listening?

I can see uniformed skeletons
hiding in the cabinet
wagging dogma tails
petrol nightmares
that milk carton our children
missing in action
but you can find their future portraits
being taught battle formations
every Saturday morning
on cartoons you sponsor

Are you listening?

Listening to their nursery rhymes
they chorus the Koran backwards
and wear they individuality
underneath their mattress
America
where are you wearing your eyes

Your wallets have cast your vote

and your bloodline fills the pen
that will ink Laura Bush's memoirs in history
tell me please
how many Rumsfeld clones have to
pigment your child's coloring book
BLOOD RED
till you recognize the rhetoric

Are you listening?
listening to the desert storm
brewing again
these Sand storm fallen soldiers
are catching oil in their helmets
to barter citizenship from Exxon
their eyes speak in gauze and
torn torsos you pause
and take a photo

memoirs of Iraqi prisoners of war
Russ Limbaugh
has pimped your freedom of speech
into a harem of childless women

listen
orphaned means the same in any language

so tell me how do you pronounce abductions
we function as sprouted CNN couch potatoes
with the launch sequence programmed
in our remote controls
surround sound death blaring from
remodeled war room basements

Are you listening to yourself
you have ventriloquist the president's speech
into your wedding vows
your paper mantras are
a tsunami waiting to be lied to

Tell me
where will lay your blame
when he is out of office
tell me

who will you point your fingers at
when he is directing "America" the sequel
from a Hollywood safe house

Will it kiss shrapnel into these
Kneeling brown children
metal eyes pointing east
salvaging their heritage from the rubble
classrooms chanting
ears ringing
Bruce Springsteen
between explosions
will your outstretched middle finger
detonate the taste of paralyzed ovaries
their intestines tangled in Islam
because they can't stomach your religion
embryos stashed in gun barrels
for safe keeping
tell me
are you avenging Vietnam shortfalls
with scud missiles aimed at the sphinx
do you think
your mangled uterus into the 4th of July
when will we try to be responsible for our actions
will it be
when the caption reads
my children died for MY beliefs
will you see
how these tragedies feel
when suffering your own grief

Will you listen then
will you listen now
will you listen before your children are
archeology finds buried 2008 years into your
forgotten ballot boxes

see the tears of widowed mothers
have quicksand desert secrets
and they whisper their
origins in your ears
but America
are you listening?

possessive pronouns

These words
are hanging in a sunrise
of yesterday beaten green
sneers of burnt oxidation
painting forever
on changing planets

These words
cause pain as deep
as blocked urethras
of kidney stones passed
through eardrums

These words
are from old Jamaican women
beating Cassava
against their husbands abstinence

These words
are of 1956
when my mother was born
of 1980
when frozen dandelions
fell ice cubes
on my baby brother's tongue

These words
are pharaohs meeting
behind papyrus leaves
to leave messages
for the future
hidden between the
layers of Sanskrit (glyphs)

These words
are of innocence
of fake innocence
Circled around

ignorant knowledge
and trivial pursuits
of Petroleum wars

These words
are of dark chocolate binges
against the better judgment
of a government issued
weight watchers program

These words
are of change
of transparent scorpions
with ivory claws
cutting human shapes
out of mud bricks
These words
are of standstill progress
and inverted paradox
of today and yesterday
of the 2 missing colors
in the spectrum of light
Forming simply Roy and Biv

These words
are of mine today
and yours yesterday

These words
are seen through my stomach
and eaten with elbows

These words
are whispered
amongst the roars
of civil unrest

These words are free
non-committal
and poor
are of bigamists and pimps

of liars and cheats
heroes and martyrs

These words
are set in the foundation
of the Great Wall of China

These words are African
with a touch of Jamaican
slept with a Spanish whore
giving birth to an American Nazi

These words
are of 1:23 AM and of 3:21PM
of reflections seen through
a broken window
voodoo and bible verses
written on the toenails
of teenaged white girls

These words are hanging
in a sunrise of yesterday
of Kings and Powell's
Malcolm and McCay's
of 125 different classifications
of a negro
during the Santa Domingo revolution
of bloodied mulattos
and diluted thought
of distance measured
in the belly of repetition
of nature's screenplay of man's demise
written on shattered mirrors
dark enough to see
their own reflection
barking trumpet lullabies
of passive forever
these words are
whale harpoons used to hunt gnats
these words are Parks and Tubman
of the United Front KKK

and the Irish liberation league
or Latin kings and Crips
of when
red and blue were just colors

These words are of Jesus
rubbing the belly of Buddha
during Chanukah

These words are mine today

These words are yours and yours
and yours and yours and yours and yours
and yours and yours and yours and yours

roots

There was a konk in the forties and the fifties
and it didn't even matter that much because
I lived in the blues and entwined it rhythms within the
roots of my demeanor

My hair
this was quite contraire to the sixties and seventies
when people shouted for Black pro non-violence pro
and all kinds of another pro's
heralding Angela Davis and red pick handles sticking out of Afros

But as I began to over extend perspectives on mine environments
I began to highlight the shortcomings of my lives
Drowning myself in its cess pool and wiping my eyes
I dug my hands deep into my scalp and began twisting and twisting
for I knew not what else to do.
Without a clue and hoping that this counter clockwise action would
make them take notice of my civil rape

So I twisted and twisted until my scalp turned red and locks began
spouting from my head.
 "Look at that dread" is what people said and I felt brand new.

So I twisted and twisted till one lock began two and everyone knew
that they too could feel brand new
Soon everyone was bound by this inherent link
and extolled the bounties of their natural kink
Creating this universal realm of robust living and freedom giving's

And I and I together felt the might
that made the once overseer still with fright
with many eyes clenched tight in the power of Black night

So no more do I disregard this extension of my soul
developed by blessed hands
twisting and celebrating twisting and jubilating
twisting and thinking twisting and kinking
Today I still live in the blues but now
I am alive to entwine its rhythms within the roots of my demeanor

then there was light part 1

They say that God is in the eye of the beholder
but who's holding god into account

They say that the fate of man can be seen in his reflection
but I say that something looks wrong with
Africa's children aiming at puberty through gun barrels

These puddles of placenta news stories are still connected
and burning holes in my psalms stomach.
so I question
how does god deserve capital letters
when his reflections are blurring humanity
when Cain and Abel hang from Newswires daily
when In South Africa Ben has been told that raping a baby
helps prevent or cures Aids
so he rapes a five year old girl to make sure
that his dying mother can feel secure with the knowledge
that he will be around to raise his four siblings

She's dying

and weeps AIDS prevention
into his underdeveloped genitals
and we think of him as evil
but to **EVIL** is to **LIVE**
in the mirror of ones soul
so tell me
how is this image godlike
how is this beautiful in its tragedy
how is this balance

Seems divinity is unbalanced when passing out pain like echoes
these boomerang worshipers come back childless
and I'm certain that if cancer could be cured by
eating the remains of day old of fetuses
abortions would be sold on NASDAQ
the fact that Africa is dying now
is not real news when diamonds are forever

Clever slogan to use when you finance death
yet still I collect news stories from the BBC
and fold them into perfect squares
so that they fit into a pocket bible

religion has become portable
worth while in small doses
but somewhere deep inside
forced together like that
I pray that god will see their words as his own

But if god is in the eye of the beholder
who accounts for the perils a dark continent
ripped by fault lines that separate men
and I want to blame them as their own masters
but they have only inherited a learned behavior
of cutting off limbs as a tribute to an overseer
100 years their predecessor

Detached hands from Leopold blades
one from every hundred African slaves
and now without rights
left to die over
and over
more over today
BBC streams seldom seen images of
men removed of their touch
Able hands spread over Cain's land
over turned on red dirt rich
from internal bleeding
Eyelids removed
Ears cut
baby's skinned
souls gutted by knives
wombs sacrificed
all for pressed charcoal ceremonies that masquerade
see no evil hear no evil mantras
attached at the ring finger

At least Master paid for our health
needed our hands to seed lands
But these our lost cousins
scream out over 500 years later

and their screams pierce
through sound barriers
flirt with the equator
tie lineage into knots
bloodline vasectomies

The milk of a nation cut off at its breast
and I can't understand why the earth has not shifted yet
can't understand why the earth has not yet stopped
this spilled blood penetrates tongues that
Have no say in their outcomes
How come this axis still spins 360

If god is in the eye of the beholder
then where is she when my pupils dance these forgotten souls
my thoughts can't believe what they've seen
and what I've seen
is filtered through eyes that could not have felt

So don't blame me for my question
don't question why my pen can no longer
script god with a capital G

NO
this is not
blasphemy
but it can't be
just me
asking

If god is in the eye of the beholder then
Who's holding god into account

today's mathematics

Tribes dance the square root of my DNA
subtract it from yesterday
cause Now
we know
multiply it with nephlim* cliff notes
extract reality ohms from fossilized cranium
superiority complexes
cause
they think they built this
shit
but they're speaking Greek
and can't fool me,
I already know
Alexander was not great until
he muffled Egypt
but that's for another day
when you finally believe in yourself
but for now
I come at ya from write angles
my acute messages measure
1/3 of 90 degrees
east praying
mantas trained in baroque street slang
cause
uptown negroes have to assimilate constantly
on Saturday nights
I tongue curl with hip hops next phase
Andre's 9000
is in my back pocket
hollah
sorry Ms. Jackson's great grandmother
built cultures
sorry,
she signed the cornerstone as
1 of 2 female slaves captured age 18
sorry
census didn't record names till 1706
sorry
we'll never know who she was

cause Jackson was the slave owners name me
what you will, erase her blueprint, but
the smell of my blood will trace
her ancestry all the way back to… *Tribes dance* the
square root of my DNA
subtract it from yesterday
cause Now
we know
multiply it with nephlim* cliff notes
extract reality ohms from fossilized cranium
superiority complexes
cause
they think they built this
shit
but they're speaking Greek
and can't fool me,
I already know
Alexander was not great until
he muffled Egypt
but that's for another day
when you finally believe in yourself
but for now
I come at ya from write angles
my acute messages measure
1/3 of 90 degrees
east praying
mantas trained in baroque street slang
cause
uptown negroes have to assimilate constantly
on Saturday nights
I tongue curl with hip hops next phase
Andre's 9000
is in my back pocket
hollah
sorry Ms. Jackson's great grandmother
built cultures
sorry,
she signed the cornerstone as
1 of 2 female slaves captured age 18
sorry
census didn't record names till 1706
sorry we'll never know who she
cause Jackson was the slave ……….

about author

Originally from England, Tshaka moved to the United States at the ripe old age of 10. Raised on his father's teachings of solidarity and pride and brought up on the work of the greats, from Garvey 'Pan-Africanism' to William Churchill, he adopted his father's intense love of language.

Tshaka is recognized as an accomplished artist and performer with accolades that include not only being a member of the 2004 Nuyorican Poetry National Poetry Slam Team and the 2006 Hollywood National Champion Slam Poetry team, but he also earned the Grand Champion title at the 2005 San Francisco and 2007 Hollywood Championships. Tshaka has toured a number of US and European cities and has been featured at theatres such as the legendary Apollo theatre, numerous colleges, and creative venues throughout the world. He also conducts lectures, teenage and adult workshops in creative writings, spiritual verse and a number of other related topics.

contact author

For booking, readings, workshops
info@naturalikink.com
website: www.naturalkink.com

other work

TarMan Celebrating his Natural Kink – *Book (2002)*
SPIT (LIVE) – *Spoken word EP (2002)*
ONE – *Spoken word album (2006)*
BLOODLINE - *Spoken word album (2008)*
Gungo peas and Crumpets –*Autobiography [fiction] (2009)*